THEN & NOW

HOPKINSVILLE

OPPOSITE: This 1931 image of Main Street reveals a view north, between Tenth and Eleventh Streets, from the roof of the Forbes Building. The canyon image of downtown Hopkinsville features E. P. Barnes and Brother in the left foreground and the courthouse cupola marks the north end of the business section. The street banner advertises a drawing for $400 in gold, sponsored by the Hopkinsville–Christian County Chamber of Commerce.

Then & Now

HOPKINSVILLE

Chris Gilkey and William T. Turner

Copyright © 2007 by Chris Gilkey and William T. Turner
ISBN 978-0-7385-5320-7

Library of Congress control number: 2007932815

Published by Arcadia Publishing
Charleston SC, Chicago IL, Portsmouth NH, San Francisco CA

Printed in the United States of America

For all general information contact Arcadia Publishing at:
Telephone 843-853-2070
Fax 843-853-0044
E-mail sales@arcadiapublishing.com
For customer service and orders:
Toll-Free 1-888-313-2665

Visit us on the Internet at www.arcadiapublishing.com

ON THE FRONT COVER: The social focus of downtown Hopkinsville has been located at Tenth and Main Streets since 1936. Dave Ferrell opened Ferrell's Hamburgers that year on the southwest corner of the intersection. This hamburger restaurant continues to serve as a draw for local people, tourists, and hometown people returning for a visit. This corner was occupied by Planters Hardware, located in the Ragsdale-Cooper Building from 1903 until it was destroyed by fire in 1927. The earlier image shows the International delivery truck of the hardware store, pictured about 1918.

ON THE BACK COVER: Today the Christian County Sheriff's office stands on the lot occupied a century ago by Williamson Transfer Company. The former livery stable building stood on the north side of West Seventh Street, east of the stone arch bridge. This structure was replaced by the Bowles and Graves Metal Shop in the 1930s.

CONTENTS

ACKNOWLEDGMENTS

We would like to express special thanks to the following for their assistance and motivation in the compiling of this book: LaDonna Dixon Anderson, Lesa Lewis Balboa, Jerry Brockman, D. D. Cayce III, Sara Cooper, Alfred E. "BoBo" Cravens, Rosemarie Cumbee, Wesley P. Dalton Sr., Mary Debow, Henry Delaney, Seth Delaney, Joe Dorris, Wayne East, Cordelia Gary, Lindsey N. Gilkey, Celestine Graves, Jimmy Hardin, Dyke Higgins, W. E. Knox, Caroline Mabry, J. Brooks Major, L. D. Martin, Joe McShane, Gary Morse, Emily B. Perry, Charles O. Prowse, Harvey Reeder, Elizabeth Hammond Shaw, David C. Smith, Roy Stadleman, James and Iva Stewart, Donna Stone, LaVena E. Turner, John W. Venable, John W. "Woody" Winfree, Ben S. Wood III., Capt. Mac Wood, Joe M. Woosley Sr., James Young, and Frank A. Yost.

All of the "then" images in this volume are from William T. Turner's personal collection. Both authors contributed to the photography of the "now" images.

INTRODUCTION

Christian County and its county seat, Hopkinsville, are located in southwestern Kentucky, a part of the Pennyroyal region. The county is bounded on the north by Hopkins and Muhlenberg Counties, on the east by Todd County, on the west by Trigg County, and on the south by Montgomery and Stewart Counties, Tennessee. This county, the second largest in the state of Kentucky, was carved from Logan County by the Kentucky General Assembly in 1796 with actual organization on March 1, 1797. The new county was named in memory of Col. William Christian, a veteran of the American Revolution and a brother-in-law of Patrick Henry, governor of Virginia. Originally, the county included all land north of the Tennessee line, west of Logan County and the Green River, south of the Ohio River, and east of the Tennessee River. All of the present counties in this area were formed out of Christian County between 1798 and 1860.

Two hundred years ago, several Native American tribes moved on a seasonal basis in hunting parties across this land in search of wild game and then returned to their homes, both to the north and south of present-day Kentucky. The Delaware and Shawnee Indians, who lived north of the Ohio River, and the Cherokee and Creek Indians, who lived south of Kentucky, traveled in the area of Christian County.

Immediately following the American Revolution, a great wave of settlers, prompted by stories of Kentucky's fertile land, made their way down the Ohio River by flatboat and through Cumberland Gap in wagons and on foot. The majority of these pioneers came from the Tidewater and Piedmont regions of Virginia, the Carolinas, and Georgia.

Hopkinsville was settled about 1796 by a North Carolina couple, Bartholomew and Martha Ann Wood. The founding couple built a cabin near the present intersection of West Seventh and Bethel Streets and a few yards north of the Rock Spring. A few years later, Wood built a home on the present northeast corner of Ninth and Virginia Streets. He finally constructed a home southeast of Fourteenth and Campbell Streets where he died in 1827.

The present site of Hopkinsville was selected for the county seat by Christian Quarterly Court in November 1797. According the county court minutes, the following year, a log courthouse, jail, and "stray pen" (animal shelter) were built on the "Publick Square" facing Main Street. The plat for the town, first called Christian Court House, and then Elizabeth in 1799, encompassed the area from Fourth to Fourteenth Streets and from Bethel to Virginia Streets. In April 1804, the Kentucky General Assembly renamed the settlement Hopkinsville in honor of Gen. Samuel Hopkins, of Henderson County. Hopkins served as a colonel in the American Revolution and was later promoted to the rank of general in the War of 1812.

The four decades following settlement produced an era of social and economic growth. County population doubled, and Hopkinsville counted 1,500 citizens. The surrounding farm community, specializing in the production of wheat, corn, livestock, and dark tobacco, established the economic foundation for Hopkinsville's growth and development. Social advancements indicated the progressive nature of local people through the middle of the 19th century with the creation of public and private schools, two colleges, toll road construction, a newspaper, eight religious denominations, and the building of Western Kentucky Lunatic Asylum, now Western State Hospital.

Hopkinsville people witnessed the removal of the Cherokee Indians from their home in eastern Tennessee to the new Indian Territory, now Oklahoma. Between October 1838 and February 1839, over 13,000 Cherokee traveled the Trail of Tears, which extended through western Kentucky. Their campground was located in present-day Cherokee Park on East Ninth Street.

Hopkinsville made a gradual recovery after the War Between the States. The large African American labor market, progressive farm operations, and the survival of prewar wealth were invested in the construction of railroads, turnpikes, homes, tobacco warehouses, and flour mills. In 1913, Christian County obtained one of the first county agents in Kentucky. The introduction of an agricultural extension service and the promotion of raising burley tobacco, joined by the formation of the Farm Bureau in 1920, 4-H clubs in 1921, and the first homemakers clubs in 1924, were progressive steps, along with the creation of Pennyrile Rural Electric Co-op in 1938.

The African American community experienced development through the organization of a school system in 1872, and many new churches and a college were constituted. In 1885, the first African American served on a grand jury, and by 1898, the race had been represented in the political offices of coroner, jailer, constable, and pensioner. Local school desegregation, launched in 1958, was completed by 1970.

The city of Hopkinsville experienced many social and civic improvements between the Civil War and 1950. A public library was established in 1874, two years after the city school system was organized. A commercial club, followed by a Board of Trade and the Hopkinsville Business Men's Association, dates from 1888. These groups were forerunners of the present Hopkinsville–Christian County Chamber of Commerce, organized in 1921.

Utility service installation included a gas lighting system in 1879, a telephone exchange in 1887, electricity in 1892, a water system in 1896, and city sewage service in 1906.

Leisure and recreational activities included the Hoptown Hoppers, a baseball team in the Kitty League from 1903 to 1954; WFIW, the first radio station, 1927–1933; and the opening of Ware's Crystal Swimming Pool and "tourist cabins" at East Seventh and Butler Road in 1922.

City streets received a new look when the first "white way," or electrically lighted street, was installed in 1918. Intersection traffic signal lights were erected on posts set in concrete pyramids in 1925. These caused mid-intersection "fender benders" at Ninth and Main Streets, Ninth and Virginia Streets, and Seventh and Main Streets were replaced by overhead signals in 1937.

Jennie Stuart Memorial Hospital was a gift to the community by Dr. Edward S. Stuart in 1914. The U.S. government erected a veteran's hospital at Outwood, in northwest Christian County, in 1922.

The past six decades have witnessed numerous changes and advancements. Business and industry have expanded; cultural advantages include a new public library; a new historical museum; a television station; Pennyrile Parkway, known as the Breathitt Parkway today; Interstate 24; and the military base at Fort Campbell, Kentucky, located in Christian County. Educational changes are reflected through the closing of Bethel College and the opening of Hopkinsville Community College, the merger of the city and county school systems, and the opening of several private academies. Medical mileposts are revealed through the creation of the County Health Department, the Mental Health Center, and the ongoing enlargement of Jennie Stuart Medical Center.

The keystones of Hopkinsville's history consist of changes and diversity. Beginning in the late 1950s and continuing for over 20 years, the city experienced the useless destruction of more than a score of major community landmarks. Each was built for a specific purpose and served its individual function, but sadly alterations were made to the original designs. Neglect and abandonment followed, and these landmarks were ultimately torn down or destroyed by fire.

Then and Now: *Hopkinsville* is an image study of contrast. The contrasts portrayed in this work display scenes of the town from lamplight to electric light, from river and cistern water to city water, from small craft shops to industrial parks, and from dirt and rock streets to asphalt paving. The lives of people in a community are partly measured by the physical structures with which they surround themselves. Through the photographs featured in this addition, present and succeeding generations may learn what was where then and now.

LANDMARKS

TREASURED MEMORIES

This image of a century ago calls one's attention to the iron bridge and dam across Little River at Cate's Mill on present East Ninth Street. A four-lane concrete span across the river is the successor to a wooden-covered bridge and the iron frame-wooden floor bridge featured in this scene. It was near this point that the town settler, Bartholomew Wood, crossed the river into Hopkinsville.

Public interest in mineral water was expressed in this well owned by L. H. Smithson, located on the Cox Mill Road, southwest of Hopkinsville. From 1897 into the mid-1920s, the public drove out to the well for a drink, and proprietor Smithson shipped bottled mineral water for medicinal purposes by rail all over the country. Only the concrete watering trough remains at the site on the farm owned by Kenneth and Sandy Hancock.

The Hopkinsville Waterworks Dam, located on Little River northeast of Hopkinsville, has provided a pool of water to the pumping station since 1895. Constructed of stone and concrete, it reveals little change between the earlier and current images. For over a century, the mill pond created by the dam has been the site of many swimming and fishing trips.

The Christian County Court House, shown in these images from 1895 and the present, has cast a shadow on Main Street for nearly 140 years. Various renovations, most of them inappropriate, have altered the architectural integrity of this landmark. Constructed in 1869 at a cost of $100,000, the building has been enlarged with the addition of electric lights, central heating and cooling, and a new roof.

On the site north of the courthouse, there once stood the county court clerk's office building. Constructed in 1852 and torn down in 1927, the building also housed the office of the county's school superintendent, the post office, and the *Banner* newspaper. This scene in 1897 features the Latham Light Guards, Company D of the State Guard. The Alhambra Theatre, built on the site in 1927–1928, was the location of a movie theatre until 1978. The structure is now a cultural center for the performing arts.

The Pennyroyal Area Museum, opened in 1976, occupies the former U.S. Post Office, located on the southwest corner of Ninth and Liberty Streets from 1915 until 1967. The 1913 image features two private residences on the site. Charlie Ducker, a carriage manufacturer, lived in the home on the left, Martha J. Quick operated a boardinghouse at center, and Richardson dressmaking shop was located on the right.

The Seventh and Virginia Street location of Kleen Rite Cleaners, owned by Jim Camp, now occupies the site of Hopkinsville's most famous lost landmark—Hotel Latham. The 93-room hotel was in operation from 1895 until its destruction by fire on August 4, 1940. Famous guests included Theodore Roosevelt, William Jennings Bryan, John Phillips Sousa and his band, Ethel Barrymore, and Andy Devine.

Hopkinsville Golf and Country Club, the community's first, was established in 1916 on Country Club Lane. The earlier image shows the first clubhouse; it was replaced by the present structure in 1953. Many wedding receptions, private parties, and other formal social events have occurred here for nearly 100 years. Activities such as swimming, tennis, and shuffleboard, as well as golf, have made this landmark a popular attraction.

Men and women who have paid the ultimate price in the defense of the nation are remembered through the War Memorial Building, located on South Virginia Street between Twelfth and Thirteenth Streets. Constructed by the U.S. government in 1943 for $75,000, the USO Building provided recreation for soldiers from nearby Camp Campbell, Kentucky. The structure is portrayed as originally constructed and now after several alterations. In 1947, the city purchased the structure for $9,500, and it serves as a meeting place for civic, social, and cultural events.

The Odd Fellows Building, left, and the telephone office, right, have identified the northeast corner of Ninth and Virginia Streets for over 100 years. Several drugstores have occupied the first floor of the Odd Fellows Building, and the home office of the Cumberland Telephone and Telegraph Company was located in the stone building. The fleet of Model A Ford cars and trucks dates the earlier image to 1929.

Students of Bethel Female College posed in 1883 on the front steps for this image. Established by the Baptist Church, this school was in operation from 1854 until 1964. It was coeducational from 1951 until it closed. The site today is identified by a pair of brick posts, located on West Fifteenth Street. Cumberland Hall, a treatment center, is now located on the site of the college baseball field.

Second Street School, later named for Booker T. Washington in 1922, served as the city's African American elementary school from 1883, the earlier image, until desegregation in 1959. The early 1950s witnessed the construction of the "now" image to the west of the original building. Booker T. Washington School closed in the spring of 1988 and later served as a Head Start Educational Center. It now serves as a Day Treatment Center operated by the Christian County School System.

Belmont Hill has been the location of schools for 150 years. South Kentucky College, later McLean College, occupied four different buildings on the site from 1858 until 1914. Belmont Grade School, in the *c.* 1920 image, operated from 1916 until its destruction by fire in 1959. The present Belmont Elementary School, designed in the shape of a U, was constructed in 1960.

Hopkinsville Pubic Schools built Virginia Street Grade School, located on South Virginia Street between Nineteenth and Twentieth Streets, in 1901. It was constructed by the Forbes Manufacturing Company at a cost of $20,000 and was torn down in the fall of 1972. This historical image is from a postcard produced shortly after it was built. Among its accomplished students was former Kentucky governor Edward T. Breathitt, who attended school here from 1930 to 1937. The 1910 Medical Arts Building occupies this location today.

Virginia Street School, Hopkinsville, Ky.

West Side Elementary School, a near duplicate of Virginia Street School, stood on West Seventh Street between Kentucky and McPherson Avenues. Forbes Manufacturing Company constructed this building in 1904–1905 at a cost of $19,000.

Originally an eight-grade school, the facility closed in 1972 and was torn down in the summer and fall of 1974. The Christian Activities Building of Second Baptist Church now occupies the old auditorium section of the school.

The Hopkinsville-Christian County Public Library is now located in the former W. R. Wheeler and later Ragland-Potter Wholesale Grocery warehouse on Bethel Street at Tenth Street. The earlier image reveals the wholesale grocery building as it was constructed by W. R. Wheeler in 1922. The remodeling of this building in 1975–1976, at a cost of $1 million, transformed the structure into the present public library facility.

2

STREET SCENES

STOPLIGHTS, PARKING METERS,

AND STREET SIGNS

The date was September 1931. The era was the Great Depression. The event was the Hopkinsville–Christian County Chamber of Commerce–sponsored drawing for $400 in gold. An expectant crowd filled the intersection of Ninth and Main Streets, looking south on Main Street, the heart of downtown Hopkinsville.

Then and now, 1865 and 2007, is revealed in this street scene on Main Street, at Eighth Street, looking west. Fourteen decades ago, downtown Hopkinsville was just a scene of dirt streets and brick sidewalks coupled with brick business houses, both vacant and occupied. A photographic gallery in the building at right was operated by the town's first photographer, Ezra L. Foulks. Today both buildings remain vacant, a typical downtown fact partly generated by the development of shopping malls.

The 1865 photographer in the previous scene turned and faced the opposite direction in this "then and now," also at Eighth and Main, but facing east. Archibald Gant, a maker of beaver hats, ran a shop in the building at left, while Hooser and Overshiner sold hardware in the three-story building on the right. The former Planters Bank and Trust Company was later situated on the left corner, and Cornerstone Communications now occupies the building at right.

Clarksville Bridge, Hopkinsville, Ky.

What a contrast! The most changed view in this publication is the Fort Campbell Boulevard crossing of Little River. In the *c.* 1900 image, a single-lane, stone, arched bridge stood where the four-lane Fort Campbell Boulevard/41A thoroughfare crosses the river today. Burger King and Super Suds Car Wash flank the highway at this river crossing.

The road west taken by the Cherokee Indians on the Trail of Tears is featured in this view across the West Seventh Street, stone, double-arched bridge connecting downtown Hopkinsville with the west side of town. The scene in 1901 reveals the results of an ice storm, a marked contrast to a warm summer day portrayed in the current image.

Canton Pike, looking toward Hopkinsville, had a tollgate a century ago. Now the view at the same location shows construction work on Jennie Stuart Medical Center in the background. The tollgate view is the only known image of a local landmark familiar to residents in a time before modern highways. Nineteenth century toll roads were removed in 1901.

The heritage of Hopkinsville architecture is portrayed in this streetscape on the west side of South Main Street, between Seventh and Court Streets. Concrete intersection direction posts, a fender-bender landmark, and a vintage Model T Ford cast a nostalgic view from about 1920. Businesses change, but the storefronts and the courthouse facade remain the same in a 2007 view.

Building construction identifies eras of popular building styles. This scene, from 1920, contrasts with the same view today at the intersection of Ninth and Main Streets, looking north. Pyramid direction posts have been replaced by overhead traffic lights, and the styles of automobiles have changed, as do all segments of one's life. The anchor of downtown Hopkinsville remains the intersection at Ninth and Main Streets.

Angle parking, as revealed in this 1929 view of South Main Street looking north, provided automobile body repair shops with frequent business. Long-established businesses, E. P. Barnes and Brother, left, and Cayce Yost Hardware Company, right, have been replaced by Schrecker's Jewelry and Timmon's Restaurant. Many building facades of downtown businesses have been seriously altered or removed completely from the streetscape.

A rare view of Ninth Street, looking east, shows the Illinois Central Railroad Passenger Station, right, extending out into the present street. New generations of trees line the street, and today's view marks the presence of fewer automobiles. It was from this intersection that the Night Riders, farmers angry at the low price received for their dark tobacco, raided Hopkinsville on the night of December 7, 1907.

An area of great change in this community is Fort Campbell Boulevard, known as the Clarksville Pike, in the image from 1938. Farmland, where the circus show grounds were located, has been transformed into the "strip." Gas stations, appliance and furniture stores, and fast-food restaurants have made their way into this area, though the anchor, Hopkinsville Milling Company, remains today as it was nearly 70 years ago.

Three corners of the Ninth and Main Streets intersection have experienced little change in their physical appearance in the past half century. Vintage cars date the scene with Christmas decorations to 1955. An intersection anchor business, the former First City Bank and Trust Company, occupied the southwest corner. Downtown flooding, from nearby Little River, has left its high watermark from the November 1957 flood on the wall of the bank building. The site is unoccupied today.

CHAPTER 3

CHURCHES

STAINED GLASS, SERMONS, AND MUSIC

Most landmark church structures reveal signs of renovation. First Presbyterian Church, located on the southeast corner of Ninth and Liberty Streets, has fortunately retained most of the characteristics of its original construction. Built in 1849, it saw service as a Confederate hospital during the Civil War.

In 1848, the congregation of Hopkinsville's Methodist Church constructed this building in the Greek Revival style on the southwest corner of Ninth and Liberty Streets. After extensive modeling in 1892, the congregation moved to another location, and this church was torn down in 1919. The following year, businessman Louis Ellis constructed an automobile garage on the same site. After serving as the dealership for Hudson, Essex, Willys-Knight, and later Ford, the building is now occupied by Bill Beliles Furniture.

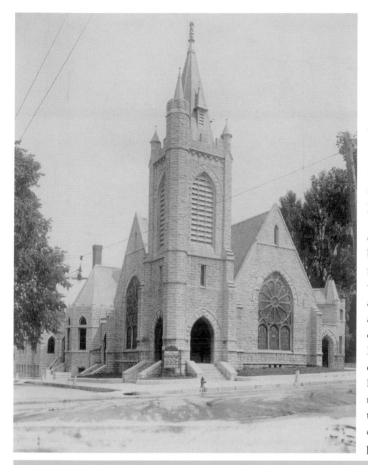

A tragic blow to the restoration of local landmarks occurred in 1965 when the 70-year-old, stone, Gothic First Baptist Church was destroyed by a wrecking ball. Some leading members of this church, with little regard for architectural heritage, allowed the destruction of this classic work of art. Located on the southwest corner of South Main and Fourteenth Streets, it was replaced, as was so often the case in the late 20th century, by an asphalt parking lot.

The congregation of Grace Episcopal Church, mindful of the gift of architectural preservation, has conducted an extensive effort to preserve their church, built in 1883–1884. Located on the northwest corner of Sixth and Liberty Streets, this Gothic structure has survived fire and a tornado that destroyed its steeple in May 1978. The 1895 image presents the same view except with the addition of Abbitt Hall on the left.

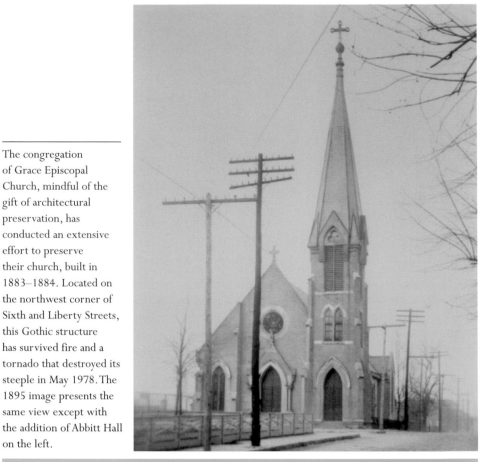

Observers today often question the church-like appearance of the Spouse Abuse Center. Ninth Street Christian Church, from a 1930 image, reveals the Gothic sanctuary, right, with the educational building, left, now painted white and included as part of the center. Constructed in 1850 on the northwest corner of Ninth and Liberty Streets and extensively remodeled in 1907 and 1937, the building moved to a new location at Walnut Street and Morningside Drive. The old church was torn down in the spring of 1958.

The African American members of Hopkinsville's Baptist church peaceably separated and organized their own congregation about 1851. After 40 years of worshipping in a church located at Fourteenth and Virginia Streets, the congregation built their landmark church in 1891 at the northwest corner of Third and Virginia Streets. Extensive evangelistic efforts have made Virginia Street Church the largest African American congregation in Hopkinsville.

FREEMAN'S CHAPEL COLORED M. E. CHURCH,
HOPKINSVILLE, KY.—23

In 1866, African American members of the Christian Methodist and Episcopal churches of Hopkinsville organized Freeman's Chapel C.M.E. Church. They constructed a building on the southeast corner of Eleventh and Liberty Streets and worshipped there until the present structure, located on the northwest corner of Virginia and Second Streets, was completed in 1926. Few changes can be observed in the church from the time it was built.

PUBLISHED BY L. L. ELGIN. HOPKINSVILLE

12693

First Presbyterian Church, Hopkinsville, K

Northern Presbyterian Church worshipped in this building after its construction in 1880. They built a new church on the southeast corner of Seventh and Liberty Streets. Popularly referred to as the "Little Church," it was sold to the Salvation Army, who used it as the Citadel (the name given by that group to their church) until it was torn down in 1973. The Salvation Army shelter occupies this site today; the old Carnegie Library and the town clock are visible in the background.

Main Street Baptist Church, an African American congregation, was organized out of Virginia Street Baptist Church in 1893. The group built a church on the southeast corner of Fourth and Main Streets. It was in use until the church adopted the name Mount Olive Baptist Church and constructed a new building on East Fourth Street in 1980. A private apartment complex, constructed in 2003, stands on the site of Main Street Baptist Church today.

A group of members of Freeman's Chapel C.M.E. Church moved and organized Lane Tabernacle C.M.E. Church in 1892. The group chose the name Lane Tabernacle in honor of Bishop Isaac Lane. They constructed a brick church on the southwest corner of East First and Vine Streets. This building was replaced by the present church in March 1958. An educational building was completed in 1977.

Members of the Catholic faith worshipped in private homes through the early and mid-19th century. They organized Sts. Peter and Paul Roman Catholic Church in 1866. Four years later, they built a frame church on East Ninth Street on the site of the present church. The frame building was replaced in 1926 by a Georgian structure, which was in turn replaced by the present church in 2003.

A group of members of First Methodist Church organized St. John Methodist Church in 1954. They bought property on South Virginia Street near Country Club Lane and built a small two-story sanctuary on the lot. The addition of a Sunday school annex and the sanctuary, along with an activities building, completed the structure as it appears today.

BUSINESS

CLOTHING, HARDWARE,

AND JEWELRY

Several local landmarks have been used for different purposes, seeing relatively little physical alterations. Planters Bank, located in the old Robert Dillard home on the northeast corner of South Main and Fourteenth Streets, was constructed in 1849. It was the location of Gordon Cayce's Antiques and Gifts from 1951 to 1980.

Hardware, automobile parts, and food have served as a draw for this location on the northeast corner of Main and Tenth Streets for over 110 years. F. A. Yost Company, a hardware store, was the forerunner of the long-popular Cayce Yost Company until 1951. Jim Noland's Western Auto Store sold automobile parts here until 1979. A string of restaurants, including Bartholomew's, followed, with Timmon's Restaurant scheduled to open in late 2007.

The famous Red Front Grocery Store opened in this landmark on Main Street facing Court Street in 1892. The 1900 image features staple grocery items on the brick sidewalk, while professional offices were located on the second floor and the Pythian Lodge Room was situated on the third floor. Currently, the law office of John O. Hardin is on the first floor, and the upper levels are vacant.

The southeast corner of Ninth and Main Streets, the longtime location of Higgins Drug Store and Tea Room, has been a landmark for well over a century. Built in 1884, and known as the Garnett Building, it has been occupied by First National Bank, Campbell-Coates Drug Store, Burnett's Shoes, and now by Southern Exposure, a photograph studio owned by Tony Kirvis. The Little River has flooded this area many times.

A popular Ninth Street feature, the Princess Theatre, was in operation from 1911 until 1972. "Talking pictures" were first shown in Hopkinsville in this 600-seat theatre in December 1928. The earlier image portrays the building from 1911 until it burned in 1918. After another fire in 1942, the building was reconstructed to its present appearance. A nightclub lounge has occupied the building for several years

Attorney offices now occupy the old bank building on the northeast corner of Main and Seventh Streets. The historical image with the stone facades dates to 1920, when the City Bank and Trust Company was located here. From the 1930s through the 1950s, the office of the Hopkinsville Electric Plant Board was housed in this building. Later the downtown office of Hopkinsville Federal Savings and Loan Association occupied the building.

Acme Mills and Elevator Company is featured in the c. 1927 image. Mill owner W. B. Anderson Jr. was then operating Hopkinsville's first radio station, WFIW, at this Campbell Street location north of Seventeenth Street. The station advertised the "Very-Best" and "Blue Wing" Flour with its Novadell patent bleaching process as the "Whitest Flour in the World." The mill today replaced the original, destroyed by fire, in 1927.

Hugh McShane the Plumber operated this business with his work crew, posing for the image, on the northwest corner of Liberty and Tenth Streets from about 1914 until 1955. This structure, located directly behind the old East Ninth Street Post Office, is now a barbershop and the office of Steve Turner, CPA. Waddell's Shoe Shine Stand, located here, has long been a favorite haunt for downtown businessmen.

The decorative lights of Christmas in 1932 reveal a marked contrast with these business locations today. Nighttime images of downtown Hopkinsville are very rare from the past. E. P. Barnes and Brother Department Store was located in today's Schrecker Jewelry Store. Successful attempts have been made to restore the facades of these buildings along the west side of Main Street between Ninth and Tenth Streets.

The landmark block, located on the west side of Virginia Street between Tenth and Eleventh Streets, has been the site of Forbes Planing Mill, the Mogul Wagon Factory, the Ford Garage, Double Cola Bottling Company, and the Buick dealer Wallace Dowdy. Early 1940s vintage cars and trucks identify the era. Hilliard Lyons stock brokerage office and a beauty shop occupy the building today.

Business partners James Pierce and M. G. Williams operated Pierce and Williams Hatchery along with Williams John Deere Implement Agency on the east side of Clay Street between Fifth and Sixth Streets from *c.* 1942 until 1979. Between 1955 and 1979, the Williams Chevrolet Agency also operated here. The building is now occupied by the offices of the Hopkinsville Housing Authority.

The old Bank of Hopkinsville building, left, and the George O. Thompson building, right, defined the streetscape of the southeast corner of South Main and Seventh Streets in the mid-1950s. Hopkinsville Federal Savings and Loan, Howard D. Happy Office Supply, Bentley's Five and Dime, and Cornett Gifts are just some of the businesses once located in this building. Law offices and the family court building, formerly old Planters Bank and Trust Company, occupy the site today.

Medical and optometry offices are now situated in the building where the A&P Food Store and Bill's Auto Store were in operation during the 1940s and 1950s. This structure, next door to the old Montgomery Ward building on South Main Street, was constructed on the site of the Ragsdale-Cooper and Planters Hardware buildings, which were destroyed by fire in 1927.

The year was 1942. Vintage Chevrolet and Plymouth automobiles were parked in front of the J. C. Penney Department Store on South Main Street at Eighth Street. The structure was remodeled by merchant J. H. Anderson, who added the yellow brick facade about 1920. In later years, the General Store, a wallpaper and home accessories business, was in operation. The building is now unoccupied.

Hopkinsville's first financial institution, the Christian Bank, opened in the old Main Hotel landmark in 1818. During World War II, the hotel was the site of the first local known example of "streaking." A beauty college occupied the building on the right. The hotel was torn down in 1960, and a local State Farm Insurance agent, John W. "Woody" Winfree, built his office on the site.

What a difference the passage of time makes! In 1914, a 28-bed medical facility, Jennie Stuart Memorial Hospital, opened on West Seventeenth Street at Kenton Street. Through the 65-year life of this structure, the medical needs and services of this community were rendered. Built at a cost of $34,000, it has been replaced by Jennie Stuart Medical Center at an ongoing cost in the millions.

An image snapped out of a second-floor window of the Cherokee Building on West Ninth Street presents a view about 1956 of the First City Bank parking lot. Everett Winders Standard Service Station was located on the left. That same view today reveals the newly constructed farmer's market, which opened in May 2007. The renovated sheriff's office is noticeable in the left background.

A private residence and a funeral home relate the history of this corner location at East Fourteenth and Liberty Streets. In 1954, Henninger Funeral Home opened in the old Nat Gaither home, which had been constructed in 1869. In 1987, Raymond Gamble established Gamble Funeral Home. It was destroyed by fire in December 2003. The new facility opened in 2005.

A 1956 structural renovation by Planters Bank and Trust Company created this visual transition from 1925. The old bank and its successors, Sovran and Nations, were located on the northeast corner of South Main and Eighth Streets from 1903 until 1998. Family court later operated at this location. The building is currently unoccupied.

A private residence, a boardinghouse, a hotel, and now a parking lot have served the town from the northeast corner of East Ninth and Liberty Streets. The New Central Hotel in this earlier image was in operation from 1925 until 1977. A parking lot replaced the hotel, though the old fire station and town clock survive.

CHAPTER 5

TRANSPORTATION

FROM HORSE HOOVES

TO RUBBER TIRES

The Christian County Sheriff's office today stands on the lot occupied a century ago by Williamson Transfer Company. The former livery stable building stood on the north side of West Seventh Street, east of the stone arch bridge. This structure was replaced by the Bowles and Graves Metal Shop in the 1930s.

A horseless carriage arrives in town. About 1902, a local dentist, Dr. Isaac H. Feirstein, brought the first locally owned automobile to Hopkinsville. He is pictured on Main Street in front of the Mercer block with his friend Tom Payne. In 2007, Seth Delaney and his brother Henry demonstrate a replica of that first car, built by the brothers.

The Pennyroyal Area Museum displays the oldest known new car to be sold in Hopkinsville. The 1909 Model 10 Buick was a gift to the museum in 1997 from the family of Frank A. Yost. "The Little White Buick," as it was known to the Yost family, appears when it was new on a road near town. Frank K. Yost originally bought the car for $1,050. There is no top or windshield, as they were considered accessories.

The Forbes family dominated the business life of Hopkinsville from the end of the Civil War to the Great Depression. Their 22 business enterprises included building construction and blacksmithing, as well as the sale of hardware, groceries, jewelry, and farm wagons. The company sold Mogul kerosene farm tractors, featured in front of their office building about 1915, on South Main Street at Eleventh Street. Professional offices occupy the site today.

One of the early Fort Campbell Boulevard businesses was Baldwin Truck and Tractor Company, the Farmall and International Harvester Farm Implement dealership. It was constructed and opened in 1952, when the area of the boulevard from Hopkinsville Milling Company to Country Club Lane was developed into the business strip. Papa John's Pizza and Save-More Drugs have recently moved from this location.

A one-lane wooden covered bridge over Little River marked the site in this 1897 view toward town on the Canton Pike. It was one of over 30 known covered bridges that once dotted the landscape throughout Hopkinsville and Christian County. It was the last covered bridge to be removed in the county in 1944. The present concrete bridge, with a view toward town, was constructed in the 1950s.

A Standard Oil service station and a Ford Exchange (Auto Livery or U-Drive-It, as car rental agencies were then known) were a West Ninth Street must for automobile drivers in the late 1920s. The men are, from left to right, Warren Fears, Norris Long, and S. Otha Colley. William D. Torian was the proprietor of the Ford Exchange. The new farmer's market is located there today.

The Mid Continent Petroleum Company Service Station conveys an image of professionalism with the employees all dressed in slipover uniforms and ties. This station, located on the northwest corner of West Seventh Street and Jessup Avenue, is pictured here in an image from 1928. The men are, from left to right, E. S. "Gene" Hancock, W. Homer Hill, Franklin I. Kemp, Gardner D. "Buster" Shoulders, Frank Smith, John P. Thompson Sr., and Wallace D. Mason. Kenny Lee operates an insurance agency in the building today.

TRANSPORTATION

The oldest automobile-related business in Hopkinsville is Thompson and Perkins Sonoco Service Station. It has been located at the southwest corner of South Main and Fourth Streets since 1927. The firm has sold Mid Continent, D-X, and Sonoco gasoline and automotive products. Several remodelings have kept pace with the altering styles of service station design. John P. "Sonny" Thompson Jr. represents the second generation, and his sons, Bill and Larry Thompson, represent the third in the business.

Railroad transportation provided the most convenient travel into and out of Hopkinsville from the end of the Civil War until 1950. Three railroads served the town. About 1915, this image was made of the Illinois Central Railroad and the Tennessee Central Railway Passenger Depot. It stood in the present north parking lot of the Hopkinsville-Christian County Public Library, seen in the current photograph.

The Louisville and Nashville Railroad and its predecessors and successors have served the Hopkinsville community since April 1868. The images portray the passenger station, left, and the freight station, right, around 1970 and today.

This passenger station, now restored and housing the offices of the Pennyroyal Arts Council, was constructed in 1892. Freight service was provided out of the other building until 1971.

Automobile repair garages replaced livery stables in the 1920s. Schmidt and McDonald, operated by B. C. "Cap" Schmidt and Angus B. McDonald, serviced automobiles from this garage, located on the northwest corner of South Virginia and Twelfth Streets. The *c.* 1918 image features the building about the time this business staged the first new car show in Hopkinsville. Today the site is a parking lot for the Forbes Building.

Barnes Motor Company, the Ford dealer, features a line up of Civilian Conservation Corps trucks, provided by the U.S. government, for use by CCC members in their conservation and reclamation work at Pennyrile Forest. These 1937 vintage trucks are displayed in front of the dealership on Virginia Street, between Tenth and Eleventh Streets. Hilliard Lyons stock brokerage and a beauty shop occupy the building today.

Sisk Motor Company, now Sisk Auto Mall, is the oldest new-car dealership in Hopkinsville. Founded in 1945 by Eugene L. Sisk, the business is now directed by his son Albert and grandson Wilson. The earlier image reveals the original dealership, located on the northeast corner of Clay and Tenth Streets. The site today is an access to the drive-up window for the Hopkinsville Water Environment Authority.

Duffer Motor Company, the Dodge dealer from 1917 to 1955, operated a used-car lot at the northeast corner of South Campbell and Tenth Streets. The vintage cars are on display about 1953. Automobile brands include Chevrolet, Dodge, Plymouth, and Willys Jeep. Yall's Shell Station is on the site today.

A long-standing Buick dealership, Dowdy Motor Company was last located on the west side of North Main Street near Maple Lawn Café. The garage was constructed about 1946, with Dowdy selling Buicks at the site from 1948 until 1960. Collins Buick and GMC Truck operated at this location from 1960 until 2005. York Air Conditioning Service is located there today.

CHAPTER 6

PLEASURES

FOOD AND FUN

The Little Chef, a short-order, fast-food restaurant, developed a strong reputation for good food after it was opened by Byrl Bullard *c.* 1925. This popular Main Street eating place was later operated by A. C. Overshiner, J. Claude King, D. E. Whitaker, Forrest L. Tongate, Cecil Word, and Bruce White. This Phoenix Building eatery was most recently operated under the name Po' Boy.

A popular restaurant and hangout for students of Hopkinsville High School was Tongate's Drive-In. The building remains today on North Main Street across from Maple Lawn Drive. It was operated through the years, separately, by Forrest L. Tongate, John T. Adams Jr., and J. Rogers Barr from 1948 until 1972. The building is used for storage today.

Little would one realize today, as their cars are parked in the lot at Big K/Kmart Shopping Center, that beginning in 1953 and continuing until 1979, they would have been on a date pulling up to a speaker at Skyway Drive-In Movie Theatre. The main entrance on Fort Campbell Boulevard led moviegoers to park in broad semicircles facing the screen, which was located near what is now the drive leading to the Social Security office.

The name of Alvin "Roundie" Debow was identified with popular restaurant service for over 40 years. In 1956, Roundie's Drive-In was located on the Clarksville Pike, now Fort Campbell Boulevard. It was across the street from the Colonial Restaurant, now Garland Nissan. Other Roundie's restaurants included the Lunch Box, the Forks, and two locations on North Main Street, both known as the Rock.

The Island Truck Stop, so named because its site was located in an island between old 41 North and the new highway, was built by J. W. Jones in 1938. After 1945, it became the Island Café and Service Station. A popular attraction for travelers between Chicago and Jacksonville, this landmark was closed and torn down in 1960 when 41N was widened to a four-lane highway. The site today is north of Sanderson Drive on the west side of U.S. 41N.

In the years between 1946 and 1960, students from the five county high schools—Crofton, Lacy, Pembroke, South Christian, and Sinking Fork—frequented the Golden Ice Cream Parlor. This drive-in restaurant was located on Dawson Springs Road, across from the Hopkinsville Drive-In movie theatre and was operated successively by Cleve Vier, Earl Cansler, Tommy Aldridge, and James and Iva Stewart. The site is across the road from where Sanderson Drive meets Dawson Springs Road.

Century 21 Town and Country Real Estate and Auction occupies a well-remembered business at the southeast corner of the intersection of the Lafayette Road and Country Club Lane. In 1948, Bob and Ann Baugh opened the popular Bob-O-Link drive-in restaurant and Aetna Service Station. In operation until 1965, the business is best remembered as a stopping place for beer drinkers. A new Ashland Service Station was built on the site in which the current business operates.

Jennette's Carport, a popular hangout for young people from 1954 until 1965, was located on the current site of the Cadiz Bank and Trust Company. It was operated by operated by J. D. and Clarice Jennette. This fast-food restaurant was a draw for the students of Hopkinsville High School.

Jerry's Restaurant, a great attraction for all age groups in Hopkinsville, was built on Fort Campbell Boulevard at Skyline Drive in 1960. This popular chain restaurant became noted for its gigantic servings of strawberry pie. In 1986, the favorite eating place was closed. The building was torn down and replaced by a Holiday Inn.

ACROSS AMERICA, PEOPLE ARE DISCOVERING SOMETHING WONDERFUL. *THEIR HERITAGE.*

Arcadia Publishing is the leading local history publisher in the United States. With more than 3,000 titles in print and hundreds of new titles released every year, Arcadia has extensive specialized experience chronicling the history of communities and celebrating America's hidden stories, bringing to life the people, places, and events from the past. To discover the history of other communities across the nation, please visit:

www.arcadiapublishing.com

Customized search tools allow you to find regional history books about the town where you grew up, the cities where your friends and family live, the town where your parents met, or even that retirement spot you've been dreaming about.